Grasshoppers' Eyes

Grasshoppers' Eyes

Poems

Ko Hyeong-Ryeol

Translated by
Brother Anthony of Taizé and Lee Hyung-Jin

Parlor Press
Anderson, South Carolina
www.parlorpress.com

Parlor Press LLC, Anderson, South Carolina, 29621

English translation © 2017 by Parlor Press
성에꽃 눈부처
김포 운호가든 집에서
밤 미시령
나는 에르덴조 사원에 없다
아무도 찾아오지 않는 거울이다
Copyright © Ko Hyeong-ryeol

This book is published with the support of the Literature Translation
    Institute of Korea (LTI Korea).
Printed in the United States of America
S A N: 2 5 4 - 8 8 7 9

        Library of Congress Cataloging-in-Publication Data on File

978-1-60235-942-0 (paperback)
978-1-60235-943-7 (PDF)
978-1-60235-944-4 (epub)

                1 2 3 4 5

Cover design by David Blakesley.
Cover Photo: © 2015 by Valentin Petkov at Unsplash. Used by
    permission.
Printed on acid-free paper.

Parlor Press, LLC is an independent publisher of scholarly and trade
titles in print and multimedia formats. This book is available in
paperback and ebook formats from Parlor Press on the World Wide Web
at http://www.parlorpress.com or through online and brick-and-mortar
bookstores. For submission information or to find out about Parlor Press
publications, write to Parlor Press, 3015 Brackenberry Drive, Anderson,
South Carolina 29621, or email editor@parlorpress.com.

Contents

Acknowledgments   vii
Critical Introduction   ix

Earlier Poems   3

   Zhuangzi   5
   Twilight   7
   The Watermelon Patch at the Top of Daecheong Peak   8
   The Seashore at Daybreak   10
   Garbage Dump Fire   11
   Poets Who Never Despair   12
   Nightfall in Indonesia   13
   Poem about Water's Experiences   14
   Heavy Snow in Sajin-ri   15
   Waterfall   17
   Frost Flower Buddha   18
   A Carpenter Bee in a Pumpkin Flower   19
   Sweet Thoughts   20
   My Dionysiuses   21
   A Letter Sent to Nae-Rin Stream   22
   Cranes   23
   Leaves in the Wind   24
   Spring   25
   Apple Pip   26
   Human Flower   27
   Noise   28
   A Blind Man   29
   Bowing   30
   Wife and Child   31
   The Place Where a Flower Once Blossomed   32
   A Flower Not Blooming   33

Poems from 2001 and Beyond 35

Unable to Go to Mt. Wolyu 37

Sinus Evening 39

Sorrow for What Is Not 40

Song of a Sad Source 41

An Arrow 42

Plane Trees in the Zoo 43

Celestial Jewel-Writing 44

So Many Stones Floating in the Sky 45

Fresh Pollock Noodle Soup 46

Where Grasshoppers Died 47

Mother's Milk 49

Downstream Poem 50

Looking in through a Front Door 51

Poem on a Line 52

April 53

Grasshopper's Eyes 54

One Frozen Tear 55

A Sleep of White Sand 56

My First Light 57

Run, Tiger! 58

Pollock, and Only This Poem Was Left 59

Misiryreong by Night 60

On Opening a Vertical Blind 61

Insect 62

Why, the First Ice Has Frozen! 63

Twilight Magnificent as an Aurora 64

The Street That Killed Music 65

Gazing 66

A Small Knife 67

Grass, Grass, Grass 68

Swan's Feet 69

A Speeding Word 70

Poems from 2010 71

Poem of Moths and Dust 73

Strolling Eastward 74

Women Standing on Balconies 75

Have You Ever Been to a Spider's Life? 76

Poem of Green Forsythia 78

In that Deep Place, the Secret Department Store 79

Memories of a Corn Beard Cricket 80

Rose with a Transparent Glass 81

In a Dead Spot 82

From Below the Lowest Level of You and I 83

Bankruptcy 84

Silver Transparent Electric Ballpen 85

Poem of One Grain of Beijing Sand 86

I Stand on My Head 87

Spiderwort's Private Life 88

Before Dawn's Ludicrous Despair 89

Suddenly I Am Passing Through a Dead Body 90

Toward Bogor Botanical Garden 91

Piglets' Summer on the Hill Behind 92

Cancer: A Word 93

To a Definitely Not-Quiet Poem 94

Roman Morning in K Hotel 95

0.1 Millimeter Chain-of-Love 96

The Toilet in Cheonho Subway Station 97

Poet Outside the Frame 98

The Time of a Sharp Knife Blade 99

Voices Turned into Pottery 100

On a Branch 101

Flower Rising in Tree Rings 102

I Commemorate Devastation 103

Skyscraper Love Chain 104

Crazy About Mitochondria 105

Contents

A Camel in a Needle's Eye   106
Please Grow Old like the Roots of a Tree   107
Could You Step Aside a Little?   108
I Am Not in Erdene Zuu Monastery   109
Looking at the Deep Blue Sky   111
Blue Ice Fish   112
Black Death Suddenly Hurled into a Labyrinth   113
Jaguar in the City Center One Clear Day   114
Grass and Apartments   115
A Counterfeit Banknote   116
Summer Devours Wife   117
My Momentary Toy   118

About the Author   119
About the Translators   121

Acknowledgments

Almost all the poems in this collection were originally published by Changbi Publishing Co. in the following volumes. The present publication of translations is made with the permission of the poet and publishers

성에꽃 눈부처 Seongekkot nunbucheo ("Frost Flowers Reflected in my Eyes," 1998)

김포 운호가든집에서 Gimpo Unhogadeunjipeseo ("In Unho Garden at Gimpo," 2001)

나는 에르텐조 사원에 없다 Naneun Ereudenjo sawone opda ("I am not in Erdene Zuu Temple," 2010)

아무도 찾아오지 않는 거울이다 Amudo chajaoji anneun geourida ("I am a Mirror Nobody Visits," 2015)

The few poems published in other places are translated and published with the permission of the poet.

This volume is a greatly expanded and radically revised version of a draft initially prepared by Meen-Heum Park.

Critical Introduction

The Korean poet Choi Seung-Ho writes: Ko Hyeong-Ryeol's poems explore the interstices of oppositions. They dream, for example, of the language of echoes born in the gulfs between such dualities as words and silence, civilization and nature, surface and depths, life and death, extinction and immortality, being and the void. Poetry dreams of the very first language, the very first expression that did not previously exist in the world and realizes that as materialized language. When we read his poems, we sense a masterly skill, a passion bringing into being new expressions by freely moulding such oppositions.

The Korean poet Kim Sa-In writes: Ko Hyeong-Ryeol's sentences are at times ungrammatical or appear awkward, giving a rough, uneven feeling. This in itself may not be seen as a virtue but once we read his poems carefully several times, the result is not at all "rough and careless." They are the words of one trying to see at the same moment the world's immensity and its minuteness, confronting that dread and that ecstasy. The apparently pointless, awkward grumbling tones he chooses to employ are deeply related to the fear and hesitation, depression and ecstasy of one who has truly seen and tried to see, which cannot be expressed clearly and eloquently.

The Australian poet Dan Disney writes: Ko Hyeong-Ryeol's poems are gently exploratory, generous interrogations; clearest among the speaking leaves, bright flowers, inquisitive children, the lost bees, mists, lovers and dust, a palpable sense of wonder suffuses this writing. In the same ways that cranes are characterized as a pair of humans —

> flying through the sky.
> Talking, listening, nodding heads,
> looking at each other

these watchful poems – compelling portraits, really – point toward the innumerable instances of our strangeness. Sometimes eerie, often surreal, these sensuous texts probe amid contours for connections between people and their places. Indeed, training an open gaze across mountains and skies, forests and skyscrapers full of human and non-human dramas, *Grasshoppers' Eyes* apprehends and celebrates the world as sublime.

The translators write: When asked what constitutes the most characteristic feature of his work, Ko Hyeong-Ryeol tends to indicate the Buddhist influence underlying his vision of existence. His poems, he says, are located at the intersection of being and non-being, illusion and reality. In Buddhism, every moment constitutes a separate, distinct reality, unconnected with the moments that precede and follow. This sense of fractured reality might be thought to underlie the fractured coherence which characterizes the flow of many of Ko's poems. Familiar moments are made unfamiliar by the unexpected twists of what follows an initial image. Many of his works evoke the landscapes of his home region around Mount Seorak, but they do not stay fixed there. Personal memories, too, shift and blur. Another word that comes to mind in many cases is "surrealistic" since what is described is not a part of ordinary life, yet it feels plausible in poetry. Ko is essentially a poet whose lyricism is expressed in a way that seems to mock and refuse the conventional beauties of lyric verse. Some critics have called him "grumpy" but there is often humor beneath the growling. In the end, the challenge Ko Hyeong-Ryeol addresses to his readers is to let go of conventional expectations and let themselves be drawn into a world where moths are amazed, pollacks equipped with strong testicles escape to the distant sea whistling, and sunlight makes a whirring sound. Rooted in the world the poet knows, his lyrics are determined to defamiliarize the world we think we know.

Grasshoppers' Eyes

Earlier Poems

Zhuangzi

In the sea there is Hwachae Peak.*
As I enter the sea I meet a boy growing old with me. Hwachae
    Peak,
fully golden with twilight after rain, where the sun sets distant with
    beeswax fragrance.
In the sea there is a sun-setting house.
Once past the coral forest, in the place drawn by the wave-patterns
    of Mother's lovely coffin, there is wave-breaking morning, home.
If you can free your heart following the wind, head westward.
In autumn with the painted decorations of Seonjeong-sa temple
    fading, autumn leaves falling, if you leave for 50 or 60 years, the
    same time passes as if on wings.
Since there is a heart in that body too, in the morning sky of a pre-
    vious life forcing out breath a bird longs to weep.
At the dawn-drifting entrance to Mount Seorak where stonecrop
    blossoms,
if you return beneath the second orange petal,
the sea encountered along a path where clintonias bloom is lapping.
The boy, who once writhed into the back of a shaded ravine,
pulling and pulling on the rope, loses his body to the world,
passes over crimson sun and moon.
On the dream shore where birds caught on hooks despair
someone alert is wandering outside of dreams, treading on night
    gravel.
Blinking in the distance, my birthplace,
soaked with early dawn dew at the top of a mountain pass,
is dozing on the desk with the kerosene lamp,
Mother called me into the mountains.
The umbilical cord that had been attached, I severed,
then I tie the aching road, bleeding alone beside the stream,
the moon sets into endless mountain peaks rising one above
    another,

---

* Note: inspired by the Chinese philosopher Zhuangzi's "heavenly wind"
and "morning migration." The place names are in Gangwon Province, close
to the poet's birthplace. Hwachae Peak is one of the peaks of Mount Seorak.

blooming with dock flowers,
flows off into a morning wave rending iris blossom
and twilight gleams on the shoulder of the western hill I left
     behind.
Mother, I miss the I living in the sea,
I suffer on the lapping shore.
Black Hwachae Peak that will surely blaze for ever;
when I touch my dessicated navel,
somewhere my mother will have turned to dust.
Let me be begotten again: from that moment Zhuangzi has been
     weeping very gently.
Before the mountain of the firmament where the sun set
the house remains empty
where once the wind could be heard,

Twilight

A boy who's been sick with chicken pox
sits all alone by a woodpile
remembering the ancient mud flats at Asan Bay
as he fingers an oyster shell.

The child spreads like red mud,
the child becomes the distant sea that cannot return,

waves' innumerable hands
at the clam-islands left after burning.

Darkness falls
and from somewhere
comes a sound of old men coughing.
Lamps are lit here and there on an island.

When the sea reaches
mother's saltings paddy field,
the mountain turns into an island, birds sing.
The songs they sing
cannot be imitated.

The Watermelon Patch at the
Top of Daecheong Peak

You know, Daecheong Peak.* You should come with me
this summer night when snow has fallen
on Socheong Peak. You can imagine it.
That large mountain is Daecheong Peak, you know,
watermelons like some enormous dream.

You know. Taking the back path by Waseondae, Biseondae,
    Gwimyeon-am,
then past Yangpok Falls, dreary Cheonbuldong,
that valley dead like twig bones,
that's the way to go. You know the way.

I found nobody, and was told that they all left for the sea last week.
If I had a lover, we would both be happy.

You won't be surprised, will you? Who would ever grow
    watermelons
on a mountain peak?
That's life! It'll be alright, walk on, feeling the winter cold on the
    highest peaks!
Walk over the frost-covered watermelon patch at the summit.
You'll be able to enjoy the red inner flesh, won't you?
Whereas if you go to the watermelon patch on that peak with soft
    warm breezes,
how much real satisfaction will you bring back after spending a
    night in an aeon?

---

* Daecheong-bong (*bong* = peak): The name of one of the multiple peaks of
Mt. Seorak, a rocky mountain in eastern Korea, close to the poet's birthplace.
"Cheong-bong" alone means "verdant peak." "Daecheong-bong" is the
highest (*dae* = big); then comes "Jungcheong-bong" (*jung* = middle) the
middle peak; then comes Socheong-bong (*so* = small) the lowest peak of the
series. Waseondae Rock, Biseondae Rock, Gwimyeon-am Rock, Yangpok
waterfall, Cheonbuldong Valley, are all the names of familiar landmarks in
Mt. Seorak, which is a very popular tourist spot.

Like sitting in a field where granite has been spread,
when I take off my hat beside the sea at Daecheong Peak,
and you take off your leather shoes too, feel cool,
that primitive state, that fresh life,
it touches my imagination.
Judging by the sound of waves in the sky,
he will surely come by midnight, and if I do not wait,
I shall be unable to feel pain with the poet.
If he says that is like Mt. Baekdu, I shall be unable to understand
    that much,
so bare-footed I leave for the peak covered white with snow,
no, rather treading on dew shining in moonlight.
Grasping your wrist dictatorially,
I should make you surrender. Do you know how to love?
One night of a woman steaming a sackful of corn—
could you, I, all of us sing with only that night?
He goes with me to enjoy watermelons at the mountaintop, leaving
    the furniture behind.
He decided to go as if asking whether the world is all my
    responsibility.

I confess that there is thought in this watermelon patch on Dae-
    cheong peak
no matter whether that is a metaphor or a song, or an expression,
I will climb up there some day
because of a plausible rumor that is no lie.
Baring my breast to you at Daecheong Peak,
what shall I say? I came for the trip, and, Wonderful watermelons!
and then what else do we say?

The watermelon patch at the top of Daecheong Peak in Mt. Seorak!
No thoughts come to me!
If that is not an empty mountain, it's a moon like a watermelon,
the wind blowing mixed with starlight melting like ice. Not so.
When snowflakes big as watermelons come falling,
might I be able to say
whether it's imagination or not?

The Seashore at Daybreak

When I see a rainbow my heart throbs,
and when I see a dawn sky
I turn into a motor.
Once the sky had been pierced by a sky-sized hole
and the sea had subsided into a sea-deep abyss,
you, some day after you had passed on
lingering in the dawn sky
understood that I was alive
And suddenly,
it's very strange, that dawn while everyone slept
bade me feel lonesome, feel lonesome.
Did you take all the world with you?
Mother and I,
my young siblings and I, we have nothing.

Garbage Dump Fire

I have lit red flames on the garbage dump.
This is no mere bonfire of old stumps,
nor is it a typhoon which carries all before it.
As they burn, that old baby duck, those worn-out shoes, dry straw.
 . . . are
no mere fluff; for almost fifty years
beer cans, nylon, poetry books, words, wallets, have been boring.
 Bottles, cows, boring.
What kind of summer daytime lasts fifteen hours?
A fallen mass of clouds, this garbage dump fire.
It's phoenix-like nonsense saying something once burnt turns back
 into oil. Slap it down!
There's no knowing if this garbage dump fire is burning or dying.
What kind of ghost was buried here? Come rain, come snow,
or an active volcano,
a sickening stench thrown away after fifty years,
milk, chocolate, cosmetics, plastic, germs,
as well as soil, iron, leather, glass, shit, corpses, left-over food,
suddenly I want to free my shoulders of them like taking off a
 water-carrier's yoke.
Here I don't remember.
So, a garbage dump, a garbage dump that never saw flames before is
 gazing at smoke.
It can be seen at a place across six or more creek banks
in a thick fog.
Shall I fetch a can of oil and pour it on? Let's sweep up some soju,
 that turns into fire once it enters the guts.
To the garbage dump! To the garbage dump!
Until nothing is left! With a large broom, a stubby brush of finely
 cut hair, a rake, if not with a bulldozer,
let's sweep them up, burn then bury them. I'd like also to liquidate
love, songs, rain, language, socks, cement, blood, tears, knives, li-
 quor, books, home . . . . home, home,
the garbage dump fire inside my body,
the garbage dump fire.

Poets Who Never Despair

Poets try to find new things,
but the world is old, there's nothing new.
Shall I seek the heart of a new-born babe?
Shall I sing of an old tree's sprouting buds?
Mountain slopes where clear streams once used to curve
cannot save our hearts.
In a world where factories' dark clouds pass over mountaintops,
drop rain, drop snow,
could anyone enable us to hear
the songs echoing from the source of life?
Even the winds of every spring and winter
that once came from distant places
where human feet had never trod, that human thoughts
could never reach, are over and gone;
only a flame of death is offered,
a foul handshake of ruin in this deep world.
Yet despite all that, just as poets try to find new things,
and need skills of higher satire,
poetry's mother is merely sick.
Or else we are poets who never despair.

Nightfall in Indonesia

This seasonal wind blowing across the continent's outskirts
arrives near the equator untouched by the fingertip of an embrace.
The sea opposite the sun, glittering once forgotten,
shines on midday in the occipital lobe, wipes up the bending
    afterglow,
then seizes the ground of the forgiving voice of darkness,
leans on the axis of extremity lying there,
and hurls a dagger at the sky.

Finally, touching your face it whispers
a beautiful, distant, humble and remote poetic wandering.

Indonesia.

Poem about Water's Experiences

It splashes about everywhere; smashing cups, it tries to climb walls.
It all the time groans, screams, conspires, expands,
shrieks; vagabond souls
splash everywhere, leap, shiver and shake, gush,
freeze, seethe and simmer, get smashed, swallowed in gulps;
in this city pure water does not exist.
Water rages.

It is impossible to experience strange animal essences.
Silent water that died rolling mad eyes in fury,
though its body changes endlessly in typhoons,
is the language of already dirty water,
restless. Water that has lost its flexibility, dawn's tense water-hues,
mass suicides of depressed waters in water;
does it fall asleep in the dry rings of southern ridgepoles at old
    palaces?
Water is being killed.

Heavy Snow in Sajin-ri

Snow became really frightening after white snow fell
in our yard for eight whole days. Then the weather cleared on the
    ninth day,
that was a tearful afternoon. Like a line not listening no matter how
    much I talk,
the sun was sinking fast toward the western hills
and at last, after many days, the village red lights could see each
    other.
I could also hear the voices of friends who had not died, were still
    alive.
Mt. Seorak used always to be dark, high, rough,
having no relation with Sajin-ri or the seashore;
that day for the first time I saw it become a hill.
The mountain, which soared arrogantly into the sky,
having no relationship with us,
became meek and mild, and utterly quiet.
The six-hundred, eight-hundred meter mountain, cliffs hundreds of
    meters high,
had all been turned to flatland by snow, and likewise the
    mountaintop was low.
Only a few peaks showed a vague outline,
and the mountain approached the houses,
although it was really just an insignificant fishing village.
Covered with white rice powder, buried in sleeping snow,
the snow yew, snow thuja, snow pine had completely disappeared
    from sight.
All shapes and colors were buried, there was nothing moving, no
    sound.
From Sajin-ri* to its farthest end the world was full of silence.
The so-called dinosaur peaks seemed to be trapped before my eyes.
The world was so small it seemed it might fly away if I blew hard,
the mountain seemed to be gazing down into the distance from
    Sajin-ri.
From that afternoon until now, I have never seen Seorak

---

* Sajin-ri: A village near Sokcho, built on a former sandbank.

so low, so beautiful like that. The sun set but for a long while
it looked like daybreak because of the light reflected off the snow.
In the village, red lamps and flash lights started to sway,
and with that Sajin-ri became a village where people live.
For nine days the mountain was buried in snow.
But surprisingly, the east sea that I looked out at that day
was flowing peacefully like a lake under a clear sky
as if somehow echoing with the voices of fish swimming in the water.
With not one snowflake piled on it, it was flowing just as it was.

Waterfall

The slight body frozen white,
once you come, will go falling in the form of bluish words.
Swelling and surging, lying flat, you will come,
so what has suddenly bound the body so tightly
to this precipice today
that it cannot return to the blue sky above?
When I gaze into the distant mountains from an open viewpoint
I wonder where my dreams have hitherto been hanging.
Flesh and bone burst out with thoughts of a moment:
Aaah! I am water without a source
and you a still motionless winter day.
On cliffs beyond fields, over hills,
today my heart's nature will return of itself.

Frost Flower Buddha

January morning, icy white, frost flowers go flowing down.
In your eyes that sorrowful heart flows.
You ancient poets who mourned over fallen flowers, today
do I hear the sound of frost flowers turning to water?
Glittering, silent, silvery petals, impossible to catch,
outside the window a morning so cold that grains of sand shiver.
In the midst of January, when only the sky and the heart are not frozen,
alive and beautiful since they cannot be owned,
you, lad, who embraced the cold and dreamed together through the night,
did you see the mandalas everything showed you
one morning when the sun came visiting the yard with the frost flowing?
Live on and never forget that bitter cold winter by the East Sea,
the ice on the window you used to stare at, with a blanket wrapped round
    your shoulders,
the silvery Buddha turning to water and flowing away, the glorious sunlight.
In those days, I had no name with which to call the frost flowers.

A Carpenter Bee in a Pumpkin Flower

Inside a pumpkin flower a carpenter bee is buzzing. Above its head is a small bee; is that your Mom? So, hey, let that carpenter bee go. Look how it's sweating, it must be very cramped. So small, let it live in the fields. A pumpkin flower is a prison. Hey, take that pretty hand off. Placing the panting flower beside your ear, do you hear the cries of the bee making the petals buzz? One bee, unable to go back, plunges whimpering through the air. As though almost dead, Father picks another pumpkin flower containing a bee. A child, holding the flower in both hands, climbs over the hill, while two carpenter bees follow it. The sea of tears in heaven and earth soon vanishes and the sun burns bright among the ten longevity symbols.

Sweet Thoughts

For ten years my wife and I produced children
then, doting on them, brought them up, taught them,
intent on taking our meals sitting together morning and evening.
I did well, winning my wife and marrying her, surely,
for without that the children could never have existed!
Never differing, my wife and I produced children
then trained eyes, ears, noses, mouths well for the next ten years,
and now, see, we're having dinner together!

My Dionysiuses

It's sure I can never drink to my heart's content.
The stomach rumbles, waste water comes flowing out,
and now I cannot eat as I would like to.
If you make too much fuss, you cannot swagger into the house
in a dark, cool alley where the drunkard god sleeps happily.
Even the gaudy flowers in your stomach
have resolved to moderate love and intemperance now.
Look up at the never changing moon in the clouds
above your head as you walk toward distant Hwagok village.
Well, I thought so! The cough-like laughter disappearing,
friends who used to be so bright, such fun
though drinking and drinking, drinking till the first bus of the day.
I see old Dionysiuses by the sea in ancient days.
The sun rises on misty, low harbor constructions,
and now the place I yearn to see is the past, not the future.

A Letter Sent to Nae-Rin Stream

The evening that visits the sky above Inje county is the calmest
in the world. The round hearts washing stones in the water
whisper, sitting together with the moonbeams, met on the water.
After kindling tiny fireflies,
they gossip about the bellflower's love affairs; still, that flower
is the most beautiful in all the world; the murmured words
turn into sudden music, go hide in the dawn sky
where the moon floats through the clouds.
When the still weeds hear the sound of the stream,
they say it will come down as dew
on the morning glory which will blossom next morning
on the eaves over the window of a youth who lives deep in the
    mountains.
How can I come to you, Nae-Rin stream,
piercing a night that is neither mist nor darkness?

Cranes

Two people are flying through the sky.

Talking, listening, nodding heads,
looking at each other.

Leaves in the Wind

Once, long ago, I was a tree.
On days when another world's sunlight passes
and a wind blows, shaking the hems of skirts,
it's quite clear that I was once a tree.
Now those vague memories are clamorous.
An unfamiliar cosmic river, rising far away to touch the sky,
turned into leaves sprouting countless,
I finally saw myself as I was in ancient times,
flapping cute baby leaves,
myself, having returned as a wind,
and realizing that I had once been a tree.
Now those vague memories are clamorous.
Azure wind! Blow hither then blow away!
Shake those branches,
telling your secret only to those you wish to know.
The old days when I was a wind were such fun.
I realized those days were beautiful.

Spring

I saw a blind man in the street.
His eyes were beautiful.
The destiny everyone reckoned had disappeared
is still there in his face.
Rather than bright shining eyes,
than eyes always looking for something,
than sarcastic eyes, piercing eyes,
why are those kind eyes so beautiful?
Neither discriminating nor distinguishing,
a blind man who only walks very cautiously is beautiful.
A face with bones, where blood and thoughts flow,
natural pleasures deeply hid,
slender hands and kind sick eyes
reveal everyone's destiny.

Apple Pip

The apple grew old as midwinter passed.
The skin is dry, so a sharp knife is not sharp enough to cut it.
The tree made it so while the apple was growing.
Inside the apple a child is breast-feeding.
In that southern orchard from which the apple came
red and green spring is sprouting on the branches,
but inside the apple the jujube-hued child
was making a spring where likes and dislikes do not count.

Human Flower

The hue of a peach flower may be lovely, still
nothing is as lovely as the human flower, a child.
Even though people say peony flowers are lovely,
they are not as lovely as the human flower, a young maid.
Everyone, turn into old men and look,
is there anything as lovely as a human flower?
No matter how lovely butterflies are said to be,
even if we say the carp is lovely, no matter how I look at it
none of them matches up to a human being.
I do not long for them as much as for a human being.

Noise

What a noise this body is making!
How very noisy this body is now!
This body in which bones extend sharply through the flesh,
while blood goes rushing all round the body,
the stars in the sky, the sand on the seashore
are waiting for this body's noise.
I enjoy the body's noise,
not realizing that bones, flesh and heart are hurting so.

A Blind Man

If I am to be born into this world innumerable times,
once I shall be blind
like that blind man.
Having become blind, I will have to walk along
tapping an electronic cane,
grasping my wife's or partner's hand,
while they will not know why they are living with me.
I wonder how many times I have been born
and lived in this world so far?
It is unthinkable that
there can be anyone who won't become blind
one day, just once in one lifetime.
The day when eyes and ears and
everything will be entrusted to the tip of a cane
will surely come.

Bowing

Today my heart
has gone to a temple and is bowing.
While leaves are being produced one by one,
it prostrates itself on the old wooden floor,
cold for lack of warmth,
then stands up, looks round again.
Myself, joyful, clean, always present,
in a forest where last spring had vanished,
amidst the final hours of autumn,
say, transience alone is permanent and beautiful.
I must come back this way again.
I must come back to the pain of fresh shoots.
While leaves are falling one by one,
in order to be able to bow to everything
today my heart
is bowing and walking on.

Wife and Child

In the bathroom beside the kitchen
my wife is bathing our son.
I hear him say quietly, Mom, your breasts are small.
Mom, your breasts are small.
In the bathroom with its incandescent bulb
my wife must have taken off her clothes,
Once the sound of running water has stopped,
my wife says, Go on, touch my breasts.
Is it ok? Of course. Silence falls.
Our son seems to be touching her breasts.
Abruptly comes a sound of laughter.
Ouch! You rascal!
You mustn't be so rough!
I long to be in the bathroom.
I want the three of us to play together.
In some distant days when we are gone
our son will remember love, for sure.

The Place Where a Flower Once Blossomed

Holding an apple in one hand, I smell the scent coming from the place
where the flower once was.
At the place where the flower blossomed, there still remains
the sound of a bee that landed and wept.
I feel sorry for my wife.
My wife does not seem to remember the calyx
where the flower blossomed for a while.
A few calyces remaining as husks are the navels of apples,
a recessed scar; time sadder than fallen flowers has passed.
How the flowers must have doted on themselves!
The fragrance of a boyish red apple getting marked by a bite.
My dear Hae-suk,
wasn't that pale pink baby flower the apple's mother?
And
wasn't that baby flower the fruit tree's child?

A Flower Not Blooming

There is a breath that never blooms, refusing the joy of bloom-
ing and the sorrow of ceasing. A radiant white breath is not yet
blooming. The breath that a breath once again becomes after ceas-
ing and blooming again on the branch is resolutely not blooming.
The breath that does not bloom though many trees make ready and
spring comes, is not blooming. The breath not blooming that can-
not be considered a verbal error, though limitless time and winds
pass, does not return. The unblooming breath that is blooming, nei-
ther sun nor moon nor prayer can make that breath bloom. Cannot
bring it into this world.

Poems from 2001 and Beyond

Unable to Go to Mt. Wolyu

—Thinking of Jua-am

Cheonnae Stream in Geumsan longed to sleep.
On the upper reaches of the Geum River, in the room next to the
    storeroom
at the Yonggang restaurant in Yonghwa, where a spoon served as
    doorknob,
with the woman who said she was from Yongpo,
with the woman who said she was from Pungyang,
beside the old table there for a full forty years,

I longed to fall, weary, cursed by everybody in the world.
Though not wanting to hear them say,
'We never thought he would do like that,'
I longed to live free of care for just one season,
until snow melts and flowers bloom, to see what it would be like,
no, until the tiny fruits ache to the very seed inside;
after flowers fall, leaves grow greener and bear little seeds,
Until I no longer miss you, though far away.

Like one late autumn evening setting off in quest of memories of
    today
by your deep body, your black hair,
as I gaze up at the sunset sky—
what would it be like?
Like a midday-spring snow flurry that briskly falls then melts,
by a stream where catkins blossom, snow melts,
like the sound of water flowing beneath it,
like a teasing nothing.

Blue mountain, what is man and what is living?
Leaving you in Yonghwa without me,
what kind of heat, what kind of cold did I really want
and leave without waiting a day?
Though I long to go racing up to the peak of Mt. Wolyu, hidden in
    the night sky,

putting it off till tomorrow, though uncertain when it might return
is the reason why I entrust Yonghwa to you.

But again today
I longed to sleep with Yonghwa beside Cheonnae Stream.
Leaving fish soup and soju half-finished on that table,
the heart that is not body, the body that is not heart,
truly, truly like that moon,
longed to stay with you by Cheonnae Stream in Geumsan.

Sinus Evening

I inserted deep within him a tube hanging from my lips.
He moved his limbs a few times, wanting to know what lay outside.
As soon as I placed the sweetest things in my lips into his body
he became soft like a blade of grass.
I opened his breast. After crushing and pushing aside muscles
like roughage and bones like threads I began to taste things inside,
things which he had stored up till now.
They were things like beads, rings, white and beautiful.
Subjecting himself completely beneath my feet,
quietly flowing into my body, he was so docile.
I accepted his journey.
Right! This time it was his turn to be inside my body like this.
If he only cast away fear which is nothing,
on a sinus evening such things would be nothing.
Like him, I could see tomorrow which was as near as could be.
Life does not die forever. Smiling in the dark,
I had already gone inside someone's too bright life.

Sorrow for What Is Not

I used it enough, did enough, and now it's neither sexual organ nor
   genital organ, but just a urinary organ.
From some time now, I have no other thoughts, do not follow my
   feelings.
That ancient, transient human way is over and done with, desire all
   gone, nothing left to call karma.
It's merely there, inside the stiff clothing, with its indifferent face.
Sons and grandsons go rushing as normal to work-place and school,
but it remains idly hanging there, incomprehensible, like an ear at
   the middle of the body.
But a urinary organ knows nothing of what it did and dreamed in
   bygone days.
The flesh which used suddenly to move, disgorge, withdraw, be
   grabbed, being trusted absolutely, unlucky in life,
has turned into a kind of scar which nobody visits, no-one expects,
   for which nobody even sheds a sorrowful tear.
A life of scant virtue, no master or book will be able to tell all the
   sorrows and deeds.
Sometimes a doctor or some such may touch and wash the bit of
   flesh,
but now for men or women who simply vacate urine from their
   bodies, it's just a thing. It's a urinary organ, nothing more.

Song of a Sad Source

That woman's thing is sad. Walking up,
walking away, that thing every woman has is an unrivaled sorrow.
Words emerge, hands emerge, feet emerge,
and just as words emerge from lips,
woman born, woman living, woman already sleeping,
women speak words innumerable as stars,
but that thing, silent, wordless between the legs,
hidden by clothes, is pitiful.
Pursing lips that never say a word,
that thing which has never complained since it came to be,
that thing in the very middle of your body,
that thing of girlhood, of maiden days, of married days,
was the love that every person emerged from.
With some flesh shaped like a bean or a dayflower blossom,
with urine coming out from inside it and, close beside it,
the door from which once eaten food is expelled,
that little thing every woman in the world has
is as beautiful as all the sorrows she has.
Today, together with all the people who emerged from that thing,
I take my meals looking at all the things they have made.
If truly the world's sorrows have a color,
might it not be that of flesh, that thing
like a woman's lips, tinged red, stretched vertical?
That thing, that tender thing might be alone,
and you want to find it because it is ever silent
as it makes eyes and love and will and heart and bones
and now you realize that thing has no words.

An Arrow

Everything is quiet, but an arrow, no knowing who shot it,
has landed on my desk.
Who can have shot an arrow at me? Have I done something wrong?
The arrow was hard, short, black, small.
At the end of the feathers, a black iron point,
seeming sharp enough to easily pierce a human body.
As I stand holding the arrow, I am filled with an unknown sorrow.
The tiny point that could pierce my heart grows frightening.
I felt stifled, my heart ached.
Perhaps this might be an arrow that people occasionally fire in fun
     toward the sky,
and it fell onto my desk by mistake.

Plane Trees in the Zoo

It stretched out its neck, long as a ladder, intending to pluck off
and eat the baby leaves playing on the topmost branches.
Its front paws shunned the grass and pressed lightly
on the ground beneath its breast. The mouth of the cool wind,
as it passes the face as small as a leaf, is the size of my fist.
The apple-shaped mouth chews like an anus. There is a tongue
inside that fist which gently rolls up then tucks in the leaves.
That chewing face floats high in the sky. I am nature's only building
with windows. The plane trees stretch out their branches and feed
    the mouth.
As if grabbing and eating the palm of my hand, my friend's mouth,
soft as a foot never treading on insects or grass, ignorant of meat,
leaves appear mottling your body.

Celestial Jewel-Writing

On days I come home after talking a lot, I shut and lock the door
and in the dark I darn my tattered tongue.
As if licking my anxious genitals, huddled in Hell's store-house,
I meet no one.
Mounting the scaffold of darkness I execute myself.
Seeds of words, those words like a space show I won't remember,
days when the formless letters pouring onto my heart will not form
    sentences.
Jewel-writing of words not even observed in the sky,
in buildings where darkness was destroyed,
on nights I come home after talking too much
I have no tongue, have no tongue.
Ice's shriek let out by two tongue-like hands.
I lie wearing a mask and stare up at distant constellations.
In the darkness, I shut and lock the night where my soul is
    whimpering.

So Many Stones Floating in the Sky

As I tread on mountain stones I can imagine:
that this was once a volcano,
that these stones were a fire burning up the heart in a flash.
But I don't know where the trees came from.
That's Mt. Seorak's riddle.
In quest of this unanswerable question,
I tread on Seorak's stones as I walk on.
All Seorak's nights keep secrets.
Their lips have been burned, they cannot speak.
Sometimes, certain people
call it their own resistance to the universe
but their lips have stuck together.
Fossil, do not speak.
Let us keep silence.
Surely the lives of the trees filling this mountain would know?
Seorak's world, where traces of spines are scattered,
burned-out teeth are tangled up beneath the bones' branches.
I tread on rough tongues, which made death's path, becoming black
    granite.
I see the souls of the light that rises into the dark night sky and
    does not return.
Raising my head, ah, I gaze up at so many stones floating in the sky.

Fresh Pollock Noodle Soup

On wild days when snow rumbles, I make noodle soup. A blizzard
smashing pollocks' livers, roes, heads, tails. Anchovy-flavored broth
with a spoonful of bean-paste simmering on the gas, circling, Seoul
impoverished for no reason. After slicing the dough I had rolled
hard, squatting, arse in the air, long noodles sprinkled with flour.
Longing twenty years long for snow on a hot sandy beach far from
home, that is what I say as I watch the avalanche flying in the sky
beyond the window,

on such days only this fresh pollock noodle soup
is capable of defeating such gloomy, dark weather.

Where Grasshoppers Died

1

I am holding up my barbed legs.
To keep them from being plucked off.
One well-stitched blade of grass,
a pair of faded yellow wing-covers,
that is all I have.
One other thing—a pale yellow underskirt.
When I spread out both my wings
if my friend notices
chirp, chirp
and that blazing city center's virulent diseases
all vanish cleanly away.
Let's go flying all together, grass-roots friends.

2

Do not feel sad for this meadow, never. Since grasshoppers are born
of earth. Grasshoppers' heads offered up smiles, surely. Didn't they
chop the sorrow of an unfocussed reception from the belts of pretty
grass seed-heads? Like a bat-blind lens. One lateral eye seeing more
than one, and three simple eyes. Jumping with the back legs, they
fly along, bump, bump, and crash into a wall. So they end up falling
downward but I, confused, am left standing before the grass.

Looking around, where shall I go now? Since all is path, believing
when told it is no path. Paths of strange grasshopper images blaze
in the air. They will be overwhelmed by the heavy snow that falls
first and last in this meadow. Snow will fall on the little backs of the
respiration trachea like a woman's shoulders with yellow and deep
blue fine cloth wings. With your breasts touching blades of grass, do
sounds like second-hands leap into your bodies?

3

Grass, grass, sleeping dawn grass!
Do not wake, keep sleeping quietly

with your cheek pressed to the ever colder ground.
Our turn to go flying off, you alone,
our friend unable to sleep,
our immortality
sucking the milk of grassroots, we long to sleep with you.
The shadows of grassblades where mountain wind is hiding,
holding up barbed legs,
have you really all fallen asleep without exception?

Mother's Milk

—Put up an awning, for pity's sake

I am looking over people's shoulders.

On the sidewalk as cars speed past a Jindo dog is lying on her side giving the breast to her pups. Because the mother is completely taken with the pups, the pups seem to be receiving the reward of their mother's momentary, brief but intense love. Mother's milk that they push their faces against, the row of breasts is scarlet. Bruised. Crumpled, panting, the mother rises silently and moves away. The pups try to open their eyes, looking in all directions like blind men. One summer midday, hard to stay alone, even, as plane trees wave their leaves.

Nobody passes without looking back. My, she's working harder than a human mother with only two breasts. Just look at that bodhisattva! That poor, dumb bodhisattva!

Downstream Poem

One of my poems longs to see the geese downstream.
Another of my poems wants to know about the geese's evening.
Standing beneath the flying geese,
they do not say they want to become the sound of their wings.
Every life, like things not ordinary seen from afar, knows no pain,
and though it may look like fun, if you say it is not,
how dizzying and sad is a life that cannot become fun.
Not so. The silhouettes of black wings flying up
into the crowns of plane trees rising to the sky are beautiful. My poems
speak and, here, despair. The height that feathers
producing wings surpassed was never high enough
so although winter's golden sunset leaves behind a sharp crack in
    the breast
and only leaves the smoke of night behind a little later,
pain is only hiding inside that.
Burrowing through the ashes left after the smoke has fallen asleep, I
cannot help but try to entrust myself forever to my poems.
I gaze at the bodies that have left downstream and are flying away
    somewhere.
Like the downstream, my river's emotions are simply drying up
    more day by day.

Looking in through a Front Door

Man is a wall-making being,
a being who cannot set up a bed without first making a wall,
a being who has to prepare a dining table on the floor inside the wall.
How could anyone climb over that wall?
If you climb up a vertical wall, there,
that maze with a roof, how did people discover
and design it? When did they realize
that I could not climb it and reach you?
They can't have imagined that. Probably,
making rooms was their only reason for existence.
So here one imagination opens anew
the wall's limits. In the first cold morning in Mongolia,
I am standing beholding people's walls.
Standing before them, I observe the transparent doors,
two flaps opening in either direction.
An unknown person pushes open the glass door and emerges.
A very old, weary, irritated face.
What corridors and rooms can there be inside?
On the walls inside the walls, what human things are hanging?
Seized by this question now,
I am another kind of existence standing forever before that door,
a being who has not yet turned back.

Poem on a Line

She is seated above a line.
young like a rookie, strong like a woman.

How did someone so young learn
such pride and self-control for life in the world?
Now she has gained the line.
She depends on nobody.

Sitting on a spot as small as her buttocks,
she turns and sits down freely on a line
and stands up too.

The drowsier the world grows, the more she unrolls the line.
She can control herself perfectly.
Until a time when she cannot move that line,
until just before she cuts it.

On that line she applies make-up then falls asleep.
Like a nearby sea, like a virtuous and lascivious mountain.

Writing poetry in the middle and consuming it properly,
listening to music, peeling and eating an orange, throwing
the peel into an unrivalled trash can,

she will spend her shadow-like lifetime.
Tomorrow is tomorrow.
She now has gained an amazing line.
The line has become her house.

All games are over. It's getting dark.
She alone on the line is enjoying games like the sun.
You alone are the girl on the line, the main character.
She is already in danger.

April

Dead things come back,
dead things come back blind,
stems turn blistered,
forgotten things that labored as flowers come visiting,
intending to recall former days of life,
intending to escape as another "I,"
intending to touch the wooden center of white death,
rise and bud again after finding water,
gather clouds, open the door, go running,
keep spreading out the folded parts,
pursue the brightest dream of life,
open up the narrow path,
put on a form that is unrememberable, unreproducible,
make one set of clothes,
find out an invisible name,
heaven and earth busy breathing dazzlingly,
intending to reconnect an interrupted path after gaining a gleam of life,
follow the path and touch first life,
come visiting, ah, after gathering motes of dust that shattered
as their names were called, without tiring, joyfully,

Grasshopper's Eyes

The caring eyes and dexterity
with which God first made you are clearly visible.

That skillfully folded blade of grass—
you cry in place of the grass that cannot cry.
With my eyes
I pick you up,
since you seem determined not to fly away if possible.

But then I
put you back on the original blade of grass.
Because of your cry, that leaves no trace, no matter how much you
cry.

Grasshopper,
inside the fiber of the fine thread-bones of a stem of grass
all alone, I
fold and fold again with my eyes
autumn, with its lament so green.

After a quick glance,
surprised, you seem about to go flying off.

One Frozen Tear

Every time my wife burst the spores of a new torso,
I had no choice but to approach my wife.
My wife was sitting quietly in the room.
In the sunlight I was completely at a loss,
went flying about hither and thither.
In a flash my wife's tiny, fox-like face appeared in the crimson chilly air.
At the sound of my wings, the mirror vanished.

Now she wishes to become some kind of feelings.
In the ideal dream of some nameless person, eyes and nose unknown,
once again, inside my wife's torso,
thinking of the situation of one loving rather than being loved,
I turned into a spore and crumpled up, on the verge of chuckling.
The face of my wife sitting in the room was renewed,
as if she had become some other person's spouse.

I am circling in the air, shivering with cold.

A Sleep of White Sand

Tonight, I'll go out
and sleep on the beach.
With a folded blanket rolled up in a straw bag, I'll go
and sit idle as the color of the sea,
lie stroking the noisy tongues of the local girls.
I'll spread out the straw bag all alone, sit looking skyward, then lie
    down.
The beach on the other side at Gilju, with nobody in sight,
a beach like that at Sajin-ri,
where the white insulators of telephone poles go rushing like
    stepping-stones,
the summer morning so long and so very hot.
Abandoning the female sea, that kept clinging to my legs, I am like
    a beggar-child,
tomorrow morning a sea of fire greener than any mountain,
morning streets beholding then running up the Hamgyeong moun-
    tain ranges,
the sunlight soaring inside the lips of the East Sea looks so pathetic.
Will I have woken early the next day, seeing Hamgyeong
    mountains,
at the sound of waters that push up the sun,
on the shore of Hamgyeong province from which the mountains
    can be seen?
My, your, your, my children, growing like trees.

My First Light

The electrician inserts a small insulator,
presses on the fragile rafter, pushes in a screw,
and turns a screwdriver.
"*Psik!*" the sound dropped onto my face
as I gazed up curiously.
Dry white sawdust fell.
That sawdust is the history
of my family home in a remote corner
of northern Gangwon province by the sea.
The place where sparrows used to live, breed, sleep,
and summon the morning.
A place where maggots lived even without hair.
One dark evening on a day with the spring equinox far off,
the red, white lines on the insulator were connected to one side of
the kitchen,
I turned a black switch hanging in the air.
"Click!" like a flash going off,
ah, light poured out! The first new light.
I have still not forgotten
that day when I and my parents clapped our hands.
When light is too bright for my eyes I recall
that baby light in a remote village,
a dazzling light with a dangling filament,
a dimness, the eyes that dulled my hearing.

Run, Tiger!

—Self-portrait

The skin of a running tiger is nothing.
The deep breast muscle between the two front legs,
the pounding heart, the flapping liver, the straining neck bone,
the powerful lung muscles gasping fit to burst,
the dappled red shoulders, the rear, with the flesh attached,
so ridiculous, like a huge bead.
The swaying brain seems about to shatter,
shaking the heavy body cruelly running at full speed,
the mind which the mosaic body is running,
the white bones looking like fists, a flower bulb like a ring,
the body full of bones like wooden pillars, planks,
the structure of a tiger racing after, pursuing its prey.
I keep looking at these creatures, for they teach about the world.
I don't blame the editors of the National Geographic but
I have to laugh at the speed of its ashamed expression
as it tries not to run, lest its genitals sway like a pouch.
This is my only window on 'the world.' That beast is really utterly
    disgusting.
Understanding yet saying: Dirty beast! Dirty beast!
Run! Run some more! Go on, run, tiger!
Ah, tiger dragging you off and making you run, go on, run!

Pollock, and Only This Poem Was Left

Pollocks equipped with strong testicles escape to the distant sea whistling. Once shepherd's purse was sprouting in the snow below the drying-racks, when the wind blew, there was one day in February when my son and I gazed skyward then pulled down two half-dried pollocks from the drying racks, tapped heads, bodies, tails with a hammer, lit a fire of straw under the fence, cooked the two fish amidst the smoke, and ate them.

The day for him to go back to school is coming. While I happened to stare vacantly up at the sun being drawn toward snowy Mt. Seorak as if I know what today is, I look toward the sea for a while, for no reason, while all alone I gnaw at two dried pollocks I bought at the crossroads on Misiryeong after spending New Year's Day at Sokcho, having first hit them with a stone to make them tender, and suddenly I recall my late father, who was younger than I am now when he died

Eager to be fatherly, I called my son and made him sit by me, shredded some pollock and put it in his mouth. When I smelled snow, the leaden melted snow in the place previously occupied by the gall bladder and liver of the pollock, I smelled my father. Rather than feeling sad, given the way I resembled my father even in my habit of gnawing dried pollock in early spring at fifty years of age, my son will surely resemble me.

The new month, when pollocks leave like loose teeth, as I spent the winter by the north-eastern green sea, beating the heads, grilling and eating them, in the middle of February the year's first full moon came hastening, then my son and I like friends together grilled pollocks and greeted the spring. Nothing but my body was left, then the new February came and went, and only this poem was left like this.

Misiryeong by Night

I park the car by the curving roadside in Yeongdae-ri,
from where eleven o'clock lights can be seen in the distance,
open the door, get out and stand there looking at the moon
then listen to the sound of a stream.
Getting back in the car again, tonight,
I start the engine with a clinking sound like when you put
a hundred-won coin into a pay-phone to make a call,
and as my body's two beams tonight at eleven slowly head for
    Misiryeong,
bending, I let all the other cars pass.
Once I reach the top of Misiryeong,
hmm, I make some noise
but my heart swells like the frightened moon at Cheonbul-dong valley
although we had no special agreement,
seeing the lights of sleeping Sokcho,
why, he's gone, no longer here.
Must the spaces between a poem's lines grow gray as they go?
I drink one whole bottle of water,
and I refrain from telling the air I'm lonely.
—I'll never think of him again.
—I'll never come back because I dislike him.

On Opening a Vertical Blind

Never think that Beijing lies behind your back.
Just as that woman does not think that Tokyo
lies behind her back. Like me who
have never thought that Seoul
lies behind my back, so outside of Beijing farmers live, plants live.
Outside of Tokyo are Tokyo Bay and waves,
and behind Seoul there lies Mt. Bukhan.
You know that too. Clouds or the wind are passing there, aren't they?
Guess what lies behind our back?
In front of our faces there is the sun, shadows, branches,
their swaying, as an endless future life
merely accompanies us, comforts us. Meanwhile
we leave briefly dried grass, a fistful of seeds,
grow gentler and gentler, then fade away.
Like Mongolian sheep that spend their lives just chewing grass,
then give their hearts, held in their master's arms.
Try to think about it! Such are we.
There is no premier, president, prime minister behind our backs.
They are simply neighbors who once lived with us.
Making our hearts low like that road,
and thinking of places we cannot go,
I'd like to say that is our morning.
If today I think of you staying alone in Seoul,
as if it's too far for me to go on account of the wind blowing today,
Far away I can see Beijing, Tokyo, and Seoul,
even though everyone seeks for different memories at different times.

Insect

You probably want to sleep your fill.
I want to do that now,
shall we?
I don't want to. . . .
let's wait and do it the day after tomorrow.
Go to the top of that high mountain
then come back!
The insect shoots up and
vanishes into sunlight
that seems likely to blind it.

Why, the First Ice Has Frozen!

Unable to hold on to a single man,
unable to make one woman wait,

when I come home at night after talking too much, my tongue is
    worn down.
Reproaching itself in the dark gut under the duodenum,
the stone lies sick, a time for being sick with hunger, with cold,
ice, water blacks out and freezes.

--First ice is always a power that grasps and hustles my heart!
The end of foolishness and desire.

No bird perches on the branch of a desolate spirit
where an empty coat the body has cast off hangs, but roots of ice
extend up into the grain of the tree again.

Only a calcined soul stamps a leaf's fingerprint on water.
The first ice, laid prone on the road, covered with dust, is the grief
    of love.
The grief of love is life's open wound.

All went racing, dressed in morning silhouettes, toward the fallen
    leaves
and the roots of teeth in the unknowable darkroom

But who is breaking that thin ice, first ice?
Unable to remember how the ice first froze as a wound.

Inside the first ice,
all the ruins of first love, what follows the thaw, can be seen.

Twilight Magnificent as an Aurora

Others' portraits

An old woman from the town who could not get a divorce walks
   down behind an old man.
An old man from this district who could not kill himself walks
   down ahead of an old woman.
They've lived too long. The two of them have contributed nothing
   to this town.
They just had children, brought them up, taught them, ate, worked.
Could any shame and doubt remain for two people who lived their
   whole lives like that?
The twilight magnificent as an arctic aurora does not look like a sad
   dream.

The Street That Killed Music

It was a moment a long time ago.
A music box dropped to the street,
tooth braces broke, clothes tore. Her lower body was smashed.
The baby shaped like a hearing-aid was squashed by rubber tires,
all her bodily functions ceased.
An earphone the size of her ear, life's lie, lay on the road.
Even though sirens echoed over the barricades,
the ten bright fingers spread out toward the sky. That city center
where her strength slipped away through every joint.
Crimson blood slowly seeped into her disheveled hair.
Playfulness like a stream of blood,
the street where music died,
is an empty, unreal road where one life's morning suddenly stopped.
Every day I cross, avoiding the spot where she died.
Like a penguin crossing from the South Pole to the moon,
at eight in the morning with music throbbing against left cheek,
    right ear.

Gazing

One bee that had come flying from somewhere
hovered in the air, legs lifted, above a flower,

trembling as if about to land, then flew away again.

A shudder runs through the fringe on the head
of the malicious star, that had been cringing like a hedgehog.

Wings beating fit to tear, a lion's roar
of droning lament and at the sound even the flower shudders, hugs
    itself
in amazement.

The sound of the bee in a sunbeam,
not descending from the air, examining the flower's origin and
    color.
Alas, there is no room to spare here!

Is it suspicion? Is it temptation? Is it revision? Is it repetition?
Beneath the bee, trembling with the wind, not leaving the flower,
    not flying down, not flying away,

Above the soil, the tearjerkingly green stalk of a red flower.

A Small Knife

I put a silver hand into my intestines and make a bud open. If it is far away, I fix that with the sunlight that went racing into the East Sea in my childhood mornings. Silver hands smaller than baby hands find a tiny pain spot in the blind intestines. In that case, I'll turn into a silver axle disappearing into the sky, and like the oblivion of sunbeams crossing a ridge of perpetual snow, I'll go walking with a painless, clear head in the morning shadow of a Seoul skyscraper. He will miss me if I am like this. A cicada is crying inside a tooth.

Grass, Grass, Grass

1

Grass has no bones. Only flesh. And the flesh is only a plan, of course. Grass goes a long way off and turns into white bones. Later, after playing with a tongue, it becomes milk. It's a matter of discarding the plan, crossing the road and encountering the body's valley. Of encountering snow as well, of course. Get through the winter, once again turn into grass in some weird place. Grass is mother, and sister. Grass knows; it loves youth, it loves old age. Grass waits. Even now. In lands of grass, when the wind drops the grass falls flat.

2

Grass whispers, "Grass-tongue!" Like liver with no nerves. Grass's tongue. Past days are ticklish. My grass loves the smell of soil. My body. It plays alone as fiber. Like a baby playing with its own hands. Stay for a moment, then go. Vanish. Make a shape then discard it. Grass does not talk. Even though the sun sets, cold mornings come, water freezes. Grass sings. Hiding.

Words of old love turn into words of new love.

Swan's Feet

A magnet is fixed to swans' feet.
It makes them numb.
When the black iron dust hidden in the soil and snow
sticks fast to their toes,
when the wind tickles their faces,
swans quietly lift their feet.
They do not walk. They flee.
Just as swans fly away in the end,
the place swans come from is the sky.
They only land on the ground for a moment.
The place they return to is
the empty, blue, deep, unending air
where nothing can stand firm.

A Speeding Word

A word, a speeding word. I want to do that. Again.
Word was not word till now.
Morning on that angry shore where
seashore bindweed still bloomed. Far off

I, one scorched sea-hawk!
A bird from a sea of flames, impossible to find a trace of voice,
today spent at sea, urging:
Did you speak, did you speak, did you speak, I say?

Like a foot longing to run to that sandy spit,
like a tongue, like the sea-hawk's billows,
bursting into my mind, a hidden word, a word of the absolute,
I contradict myself. At this moment . . .

Poems from 2010

Poem of Moths and Dust

The moment the window is open, moths go flapping up, beating at
    empty dreams.
Moths drunken with sleep shake the dust from their wings in all
    directions.
Just as meteoric sparks and motes of dust go flying,
the room suddenly wakes from astonishing sleep. Dandruff of
    weary life,
the moths are all amazed that we were asleep in a place like this.

The moths' wings rustled like perilla flowers, like the ovaries enclos-
    ing perilla seeds,
again and again at the far end of my eye.
The moths, unable to find safe branches or eaves in the air, re-
    mained floating forever,
touching and flapping little wings like the eyes of darkness.
I disliked having the degenerate moths' eyesight probing my eyes. A
    morning
when dark pupils with nothing else were open inside my eyes,
I tried thinking that the pit was drifting in the void.

That morning I turned into a moth. Brushing off its wings, that
    could not evolve,
the moth looked for the lamp but the lamp had been turned off at
    midnight.
Once the light was off, the moths became unable to find the
    darkness.
Therefore, fluttering their wings, they wandered about in the void.
As dazzling morning sunlight shone into a small basin in the
    mountain,
unexpected moths rose like dust behind the curtain, opened
    carelessly.
This is my unhappy morning song for today.

Strolling Eastward

When he hums I grow tense.
He turns up once each time by this lonely easterly downward
    stream.
The brook leads to the sea and meanwhile the mountain
ceaselessly vomits gravel downstream.

He is humming. Hands deep in his pockets,
not disturbing anything, he walks alone along the byway.
Along the byway, dewdrops, and little insects that watched all night
    long,
a path always connected to faint glimmerings of light.

There is nothing as free as his humming.
There is nothing as political as his humming, but
above all there is nothing as futile as his humming.
I call out to him, there on the ground, and, at the same time, beside
    the stream,
downstream and, at the same time, on the mountaintop.

He has no dealings whatever with Mother Nature.
He merely walks along a very tiny path inside.
Still, his humming has a charm beyond greatness,
a person conscious of being a weak existence.

He turns back at the spot where the river makes a bend
Before that, he sits there briefly, looks, listens to the water.
The pebbles gathered on the stream's floor gaze at him.
The faces of the icy stones were inside him.
He turns back, muttering this phrase.

Just as when he was walking downstream, without any change,
he comes back with the same humming. As if nothing had happened,
behind his back the crimson ball of dawn follows him.
Once he does a tap-dance down that path,
then starts to hum again quietly
For him, reality is always too fearful a place.

Women Standing on Balconies

A woman jumped from her apartment.
An investigation is under way as to why she jumped.

I have no idea what use they will make
of their investigation of the woman who jumped.
The police set up a police line. As it flutters in the breeze, death
resembles an everyday weakness turning into lies in the presence of life.
One thing is perfectly clear:
the fact that one woman in Seoul, Korea, unable to control herself,
has put an end to her life.

Well, it might be a conflict between desire and obsession.
In any case, one woman in this country died
after jumping from the apartment she and a man had set up together.
Around midday all the local inhabitants simultaneously
heard the sound made by that woman falling with a thud on the
    sidewalk.
The womenfolk remember hearing a really sickening sound
as the woman crashed to the ground.

For every woman there is the possibility of falling
and the risk of jumping from their apartment.
Apartment blocks are so high and vertical. Young women
grow plants and flowers on the balconies of that same block.
Thinking of their own women, they water plants and flowers.

Just as they are hanging up washing on the balcony, or inadvertently
    moving a flowerpot,
slowly or in a flash a change can happen.
The only place women could fly into, the only place women could
    jump down from
would be the balcony stuck outside the block.

Perhaps Korean women so resemble the balconies
that Korean women standing on balconies are anxious.
Women lingering on balconies are at risk.

Have You Ever Been to a Spider's Life?

After endless difficulties, our family of four crossed the threshold.
We had lost Father. We went into a room.
We were stunned. One faint light bulb was dangling from the middle
    of the ceiling.

The wire shook occasionally in the wind coming from outside.

As we stared up at the bulb, we were walking across a reed mat.
On the other side we could see a red clay wall through the torn wall-
    paper; we were heading
in that direction when we heard a buzzing sound of wind like
    memories.
In the tubes of our ears, fine as hairs, the wind made a sad sound.

Everything made a sound like that as it passed.

We do not know what kind of season humans are passing through
but in that room one man, like an elderly student,
was reading a black book. We were passing
directly beneath the man's bookcover.

With his head seemingly tilted back, the rather gaunt man suddenly
    moved.
He must have glimpsed Big Brother going before him. The man
swept up Big Brother, threw him outside, and returned to his book.
Mother walked across in front of him. She stood on the spot
where her son had vanished and looked around.

Just then the man swept Mother up, opened the door and threw her
    outside.
She went flying like a grain of dust. The man
laid a thin sheet of paper over Younger Brother as he followed behind,
as if forcing him to seize it in his mouth.
Younger Brother climbed on top of the paper. Just then the man
opened the door and threw him outside.

Standing behind him, I screamed and wept. It is hardly likely
that he heard me
but the man seemed to sink into some kind of deep thoughts.

I have no idea what became of my kith and kin after that.
There was a sound of wind blowing all night long. In the dark
from beneath the reed mat I silently observed him.
Vague thoughts went passing by. There was no idea
that those passing thoughts were sad.

This was our family's future history.
The man had only thrown the spiders out, without killing them,
but that night I made my way into the clay wall behind the torn
    wallpaper.

Poem of Green Forsythia

They say that if you go somewhere in North Chungcheong province,
there are many white forsythias growing.

They say those girls have names like ivory forsythia, pink forsythia,
    round forsythia,
and among the rest is a green forsythia, they say.

Endlessly, in spring, too, called green forsythia, in summer, too,
    called green forsythia,
still, now, when winter snow is bad, green forsythia
is always its own forsythia, never becoming my forsythia, it seems.

Neither as tall as a school-yard tree, nor as precarious, just one meter
    high,
green forsythia is not very fragrant,
and though it always grows on slopes,
it seems it has no idea why it is known as green forsythia.
There, it produced countless insipid buds and vascular bundles
and that endless all-seasons repetition alone was its joy while living in
    the mountains.

Purple, glossy flowers bud on the branches of maid-like green
    forsythia,
green forsythia that first produces blossom the following year,
yet nowadays, they say, green forsythia is gradually vanishing.

They say that somewhere on a hillside in North Chungcheong
    province
green forsythia is still growing.

In that Deep Place, the Secret Department Store

That woman seems not to realize with what difficulty I am breathing.
That woman will never have heard the sound of my breathing.
Every man employs violence against this breathing sound
then grows angry at that violence.
However, perhaps because women have chosen extremely simple
    results,
complex procedures are off-limits to female consumers.

Apnea iron hidrosis speeding into a dark tunnel,
the jockey lashes the bulky rear of the black, gorgeous racehorse with
    his whip.
Blood oozing out and gathering in the clinging traces of the whip,
scatters at the speed of light.
The breathing sound of the racehorse, blood flowing in the dark as it
    gallops on, screams.
The black hairs growing inside the windpipe's bend are being sucked
    inward.

After that, if the woman hears the sound of my breathing, she will sum-
    mon me
and force me to purchase disgusting love. What arouses desire inside
    women
is the light of that department store. The woman has no idea of where
    she is breathing.
Like the hidrosis inside the tunnel developing as a bad habit.

Memories of a Corn Beard Cricket

The corn beard cricket
is quiet when the 80-floor elevator is going down.
It stops chirping and the elevator listens to the hum of its engine.
Sometimes, things not up-to-date tend to make signs.
The beard cricket is near the iron beacon.
The hum of the engine enters its grass-blade breast
and vanishes as if from a seahorse.
In the seahorse traces of memories remain like waterdrop-dust.
The sound has vanished and is already no longer there.
The sound of the 80-floor elevator-chain swishing can be heard
    through the walls.
Technology is making every effort to conceal that sound.
When my newspaper-like face is lit up by the sensor,
the door quickly opens sideways like a secretary; then,
standing aside, waits for me to go out.
If I do not go out, the door remains standing like something unsettled.
Then sunlight touches the blue veins on the back of my hand.
The cricket is beginning to chirp like a late-summer cicada.
Suddenly, with the remoteness of a slight fever,
I grasp the glass window with my palm. One autumn cloud
floating above the hill behind the apartments is ablaze.
I hope the last fiery canna will adorn itself brightly.
One beard cricket like initial cancer of my alveolus
began to chirp in the last beams.
I want to see, want to touch your name,
corn beard cricket.

Rose with a Transparent Glass

The bottom of a rose vomits muddy water.
The water in the vase began to grow turbid.
The green stem continues to vomit.
The foolish rose stalk tries to suck up
that water once again.

Already, in times gone by,
the rose absorbed every ignominy.

There is nothing left for the rose.
The thorns open the blood-stained eyes of morning.
Beside the rose, sunlight is bleeding.
Before morning sunlight passes through the window
the rose raises the glass, intending to drink the water.

In a Dead Spot

I suddenly ended up entering a dead spot with no signal.
I read the patterns on the leaves that have locked the door of the
  noisy world.
You briefly look around; are you seeking missing feelings?
The zone with no signal of soundless chlorophyll,
a region where the cries and movements of animals are not
  detected,
is a territory corresponding to an area of non-aggression for us,
the uproar of communications confuses even small meditations.
I throw the key in my pocket outside of there.
When the ring opens and wings flutter, just then
I lose the chance of calling their names.

Therefore, I vanish from the distant memory of ribosomes.
From within the unexpected substratum said to integrate
  mountains
by the notion of plant conservation area, I see outside the region.
Standing shadows with contorted faces
after smearing their faces with something on their palms stood
  eavesdropping.
Now I have a unique dead spot.
Here all communications of disorder have been cut off.
Light having left, on one side of the darkness where chaos went
  walking,
in a spot completely dead, without any signal, you and I
are quietly touching the fact that we lost one another long ago.

From Below the Lowest Level of You and I

At the very lowest, basic level, you can see straight.
At the very lowest, basic level, you can call my name, for sure,
or maybe you can call the name's me.
At your lowest basic level, the level with nothing underneath,
a basic level lower than the bottom of a ship, the palm of a hand, the
    sole of a shoe,
you could reveal wholeness before my eyes, for sure,
after having gained the lowest level, and then after the next to the next
    to the next,
in this void one muddy day when rain strikes the fence,
I'll be able to arrive alone at your snow-white basic level, for sure.
I'll be able to put my black basic level on your's, for sure.
In order to feel that snow-white basic level from my basic level,
gathering all my strength, I'll manage to support my basic level, for sure.
Like white bearings rotating at high speed,
contrast, can you touch my lowest level for sure?
Conveyor belt crossing over, striking and waving
a slippery barb stuck to the lowest level,
will I be able to say here is indeed that death?
I am hanging upside-down from your lowest level.
Now I coincide with the inside of the lowest level.

Bankruptcy

Opening my eyes one morning, I found I was unhappy.
My wife, who had cleaned off her make-up about midnight
was enjoying a lie-in, asleep with her legs stretching down the bed
and the children had gone out to the riverside park.
Refrigerator and washing machine, television set, surrealistic picture,
come to think of it, all the property I have accumulated seems
to come down to nothing more than such things.
The day when the orders of the bankruptcy court were completed,
I couldn't open my eyes.
The way all my professing, studying, marrying, birthing
had stopped here just like that.
My morning was too heavy and dark.
My last morning in this Seoul was appalling.
I can't count them, all the people related to me involved.
I can't tell how hecticly I have been living.
suddenly a cry shook me, as though expelling some kind of filth.
My bankruptcy, which I couldn't remember, couldn't make up for.
I cannot remember myself after that.
I left no will for anybody. From today
I am simply an absence having no relation with this city.
From somewhere a sound of waves echoed, fell silent.
I realized that on that earth I was being abolished.

Silver Transparent Electric Ballpen

I never use a silver transparent electric ballpen.
When I push a flower button with an index finger, it sends a blue
    light signal
into the eyes in the brains of the children;
when I touch the back of a rubber sheet, a pink light shines and
    smiles at me.
The yellow ring of the very, very tiny doll of an axis
that can only be seen if you look closely, as it turns,
cries sparklingly like an electric top.

Inside that, a child is sitting on a swing.
Every time I touch the silver transparent electric ballpen,
eyes and heart light up brightly, pink and blue, becoming the origi-
    nal child.

For fear that the light from the silver transparent electric ballpen
    might fade away,
the child has set off into the glass window
and the silver transparent electric ballpen alone remains.

Only the silver transparent electric ballpen left behind under that
    world is to be remembered.
The silver transparent electric ballpen made by little angels' hands,
the silver transparent electric ballpen played with by children's hands.

Poem of One Grain of Beijing Sand

—January 2008, for Changming Xia

One sand grain is shaking.
The other man who slept there is still lying on the bed.
The early morning sunlight is making a whirring sound.
Hearing that noise, the man sees a Tibetan custom.
My eyes are like a thin film of jelly, like a dog's eyes,
A dog's eyes are clearer than human eyes.
The man is operating the washing machine, boiling water.
The sand grain resembling me moves briefly.
It scolds the lazy man who does not focus on it.
Your morning! What are you looking at now?
So, Beijing wind, I have become your sand grain.
Someone lying on a high-rise bed is looking down at me.
Your concern lies in never taking any rest.
Now the sand grain of artificial eyes is becoming me.
I cannot tell where I am now. Now I
am shedding tears like sand grains.
There, over there, a tear-like sand grain is shaking.
The sand grain is not wet like tears.
Riding a car decorated with thin threads, the man calls to the man
but the sound is unable to pierce the door of the room and go inside.
The sand grain alone is shaking before my eyes.
Like a mirage in the desert not far from the Beijing bed,
like a sand-laden wind, like the man's eyebrows, Beijing!
You'd better roll the sand grain at least one step ahead of me.
In order to glimpse a self suddenly changed in a flash,
it is not right to stop like that for a whole generation
on a cold morning in a single spot.
Crystal-hued sand grain like Beijing's dreams!
Still the sand grain shakes,
the sand grain is right before my eyes. In my dry eyes
the sound of the wind brushing past the sand grain can be heard.

I Stand on My Head

Father enjoys standing on his head.
Father began to stand on his head some time ago.
Raising his legs high in the air,
he pays no attention to us as we watch from behind.
His heels do not even touch the wall.
Seeing him, we laughed, called him Upside-Down Father.
Father spends all day writing something at his desk.

If we forget about him, then look round on hearing him exclaim,
Father
is infallibly standing on his head. Several times each day
he stands on his head in order not to forget how to stand on his
head.

Recently the time he spends standing on his head has grown longer.
The rest of the family has no interest in Father standing on his
head.
Maybe our house will disintegrate before long.
Our house is a house where Father is tirelessly writing something,
a house where Father stands on his head.
What on earth is Father writing down like that?
Some day Father will just die while standing on his head.

Yet Father is watching us intently.

Spiderwort's Private Life

It crawls and spreads by growing creepers. With no good-will
an unknowable lust went crawling ahead.
Children, suspended at the end of its stalks, shudder.
Open-eyed, seeing nothing,
in a place where nothing is visible,
or like a dog barking in the dark,
the spirits of its green stalks went in single file.
Not so much as dreaming that after breaking the knee
the lips of the water would touch the air and return
it was unable to go beyond the lower limit of the nival zone
but after hiding beneath the brook, they
puffed out dazzling mouths with empty stalks.
In those days, mists and air were like lovers.
An over-secretive, light-weight relationship
like the colorful buds and purple flowers of spiderwort
scattering the surroundings by whispers
left it alone to learn.
Faster and lighter than a racing car beyond the bank,
more detailed and stronger than the sun's line of latitude,
able to occupy the place where we are supposed to be,
it spread out an unbreakable first lust.
Night came, when I could apply soap to my hands
in order to wash away that grass-juice.
Shaking together like a spring, noise
of the unforgettable, furtive pleasures of the spiderwort,
I approach you, sitting there.

Before Dawn's Ludicrous Despair

Setting a light in the dawn sky, he writes poetry.
Writing poetry, the act of erasing something,
like pain contained and confined in the blood,
the soul's iterative, never erased no matter how he tried,
he wishes never to experience that living moment.
Like peeling away the flesh with sandpaper, performing a lasik op-
    eration alone,
behold that deformed man setting a light in the sky till dawn
and dreaming dreams of language.

Unaware how ludicrous such insomnia is,
the wall of blood-red despair that poetry cannot reach,
even if blood-like scrap paper is held in fresh hands,
does he know a penetration darker than dawn, inwardly
illusory messages stuck hanging in the air, unable to descend?
Finally the man will arrive at dawn.
Demolishing a mountain full of cuts and bruises,
into the unexpected absence of language, unable to embody
    anything,
as if tumbling, as the first subway train passes below.

Suddenly I Am Passing Through a Dead Body

It's only when you're laid out that this society grows quiet.
It's only when you're dragged along the ground that the pain stops.
Unconsciousness overthrown by the gigantic face's teeth,
the body pounced, and as the Adam's apple bitten broke
I collapsed below the breast. After dragging me under the trees' shade
he began to kiss my whole body.
Saws and hammers were attached to his mouth.
I listened to the sound of his biting beneath the heartbeat. *Munch,*
     munch, munch.
He munched at the soft, long intestine.
I was watching him open-eyed.
Did they thus come across, get trained, and after becoming deep and
     being forgiven,
then make the city's skyscrapers and sewers, I wonder?
The fear anticipated when crossing into another life after passing
     through darkness
you, prostrate, your stomach stuck to a rock as satiety,
the face of Yama, King of Hell,
rubbing, pushing, mixing soft guts,
is that foul drowsiness from somewhere far off coming to visit?
We, turned into guts, somewhere with anonymous,
bloodstained fat will whitewash bruised intestines,
embracing the face of another life, a meadow looking forward to
     Hell's summer,
massaging a dead body as if chewing and swallowing a piece of meat
you are passing my abdomen by the light of your own eyes.
What will you call the present me, gazing down at you like a cloud?
What year, month, day, hour, as of now?

Toward Bogor Botanical Garden

Tidings came from Bogor botanical garden,
saying that a man had appeared in Bogor botanical garden,
a green door had opened and he passed through.

I can never go to Bogor botanical garden.
I do not know what flowers are blooming
in Bogor botanical garden.
Tendrils and Bogor botanical garden are far away.

Having lived then died in Bogor botanical garden, he
knows the pleasure of the *ālāya* time which must be announced,
that vanishes in the time of plants.

By not measuring useful human time
Bogor botanical garden is peaceful.
Beyond the horizon meeting the bright tropical night, beyond
hours that do not heal themselves

So long as plants live and die like humans
there is no blood-line in a plant's family tree.
Wind and water have nothing to do
with human exploration and speech.

If I go to Bogor botanical garden I am vanishing.
Suddenly, someone coming close to plants again
becomes an unfamiliar, scale-like leaf.

I wave my arms in the sky. Like a book,
sprouting, I stand erect
beyond the morning I head for Bogor botanical garden.
As dream, as leaf, as wind, as indifference.

Piglets' Summer on the Hill Behind

Last Stroll in Seoul

Below the bank where hogweed and spiderwort were flowering
piglets roam grunting. They dig and bore through the soil
and as a result their mouths have grown like hands, their hands like
     mouths.
Busily doing something or rather nothing,
flapping red ears, their noses keep snuffling. Every day I
go up the hill behind the house and check how the pigs are doing before
     going down.
Cute piglets, roundly oval mouths with teeth and tongue,
maybe not first-class products
but beneath the bank thick with spiderwort and hogweed
the pink-fleshed piglets play with water and wind before they disappear.
Now they are poised to leave, borne on the wind.
Noticing that, I often visit the spot.
They take no notice of my coming and going.
I like that. When leaves start to fall, soon, their numbers will shrink,
and once damp, chill winds blow from far away
I'll not be able to see lovely pigs' rumps for quite a while.
Then next spring,
like grass, they will emerge and again roam around grunting loudly.
I hope you realize that they are a sound
never transgressing others' territories, content to roam around their own,
then again, like this autumn, returning . . .

Cancer: A Word

In a Seoul hospital

That woman has been lying sick in bed for a hundred days.
As the fishing line tugs at the network of nerves within her flesh,
she gradually transforms into a bed.
It's hot, flowers of a thousand tons of pain are blossoming.
Her little tongue alone is alive, as if stabbing her body all over.
Her body is the size of a cat's tongue.
She contemptuously spits out death's agonies.
Death fights to forget fear.
In a room painted with bone-wrenching struggles
on the bed bullets explode, spears rise.
The woman is becoming a slave. Pressing down the bones
like a piano keyboard that makes sounds when pressed,
the four-cornered bone's bed bearing the pain,
the woman utters sticky shouts,
the battered body torn to shreds.
When you die, spit out your cursed body.
The hundred and first day, dreadful as a nightmare,
with each and every word cutting into the bones,
a high-rise crane raises up the woman's bones.
Lifts high the reinforcing bars.

To a Definitely Not-Quiet Poem

Nowadays I do not cultivate quietness.
I take noise as my principle.
Weak-sighted, I open huge ears
amidst the noise and write poems.
Those ears are like the ears of demons
but with the noise erased I am an empty shell.
Like the 2,500 gold-hued pagodas at Bagan,
silence listens to the noise in this city,
located in the opposite direction to autumn's trajectory.
Not today, but since yesterday
I write poetry amidst noise. Therefore
for me only noise is the proof of reality.
A place with no noise is a dead place.
I summon noise, write noise.
In the absence of noise, language grows uneasy,
my poems don't progress.
Taking silence with me, I set off in quest of noise.
In order to associate with noise, in order to live
with noise, amidst noise,
I reply on demons' ear-flaps.
Unable to afford to lose that light, I
try to return noise to language.
Silence is a form concealing noise;
I can write nothing in darkness
Amidst noise, words are active without a moment's leisure.
Between truly florid noise and noise
a bundle of breath binding up language;
amidst noise my poems grow more elaborate.

Roman Morning in K Hotel

I wished I had not woken from sleep.
I wished people's voices were inaudible
Like those plants or the air in the street behind the hotel.
Jewel-like poems and crimson tulips
are somewhere too remote for me.
I did not want to hear the morning call.
I wished morning had passed by like the sound of cars
through the city-center with its labyrinth-like unfamiliar streets.
I wished my fingertips had not woken.
I wished not one single memory had visited my body.
Suddenly all the things I wanted to do vanished.
That's what it whispered to me.
Taken by surprise, I listened carefully to my words.
With my face buried in the bed-sheets.
Then torn branches and branches became visible.
For no reason my body wanted to wail.
With the moon hanging upside-down in the window.
On the inside of a fortress with noisy sunshine.
Even if I cannot sustain every pain.
One strange man in the mirror.
Since I shall never be able to return to this morning.
I am now standing before the mirror.
Roman hotel, stationary that morning.

0.1 Millimeter Chain-of-Love

The chain-of-love creeper takes precautions against every 0.1
    millimeter.
Without stretching forward, the love-chain nibbles at the void.
It knows that the void does not belong to it.
The love-chain is not willing to cross over, if it is allowed not to.
Not invading other regions is a principle.
From behind, people say the love-chain is timid.
Would it be easy for the love-chain to stretch forward without mass
as it crosses the room on a spider's web?
But the love-chain does not expand itself.
The love-chain's dread focuses on controlling growth.
Its leaves are smaller than a shirt-button.
Life's will is dependent on a desperate urge not to grow larger.
Wire-like 0.1 millimeter love-chain's agony.

The Toilet in Cheonho Subway Station

It was cold. Dashing into the toilet, I stood there.
A stabbing headache came, from the urinal.
Ah, the sexual lust and homicidal intent of this tedious sorrow.
An urgent sense of having to live remained here.
The stench of urine pricked my nose and flew into a rage. Part of
    the sorrow froze.
The stench of Seoul smelled after a while in an early-winter toilet.
A morning when one guy after another finished urinating and went
    sprinting off;
bodily waste vanishing hurriedly after being roughly wedged into
    the waistband,
for some reason, today, feeling like a winter terrapin, still and
    desolate.
The weird toilet, where urine smelled like an ointment, a lingering
    hangover,
had a stench that smelled sweet.
The worm-sized flesh-hole opening sufficiently
for the quantity and temperature of what was being expelled.
The cold encountered on the way to exit 6
of Cheonho subway station leading to Hyundai Department Store,
making the long urethra journey to the urinal like dirty earwax,
a 2005-style toilet, smelling of ammonia,
linked to kidneys, veins, urethra, that toilet with its heater,
I taste no discharge, before the urinal, flesh thrilling,
severing the tongue, displaying the guts, living,
people vanishing, raising their coat collars
in a futile attempt to keep the wind from their ears.
Hey, wife, the tip of my willy's hurting.

Poet Outside the Frame

One man did all he could to get inside a frame.
The frame refused to receive a poet. Painless times? Forget it!
People dying is not just a modern problem.
The conflictual relationship of boredom and desire,
in fact, all truthful beings dream of getting into a frame.
Nothing but a common pose performance, but lying pains reign.
In these lies, everything is invested and rejected.
The dead smile at us from inside the frames beyond the present.
In glass fiber, speeding along a fine fiber optic cable
he suddenly exclaimed.
Is it alright to hang the frame on a wall and get into it? Is it alright
to climb into the frame head-first with your shoes on?
Or taking off your socks and holding them? Or
did you cut off the lower part and only frame the upper part?
There is peace in the frames of odd writers whose faces alone went in,
as they wrote one single line.
From inside the frames they look out, holding the edge of the frame.
Am I too fat to get into that dazzling frame?
December, snowflakes flutter on the frame,
peaceful like a drink on the coldest day.

The Time of a Sharp Knife Blade

A knife like a shoe horn, knife like a trumpet, knife like a bottle,
    knife like a branch,
after going inside my ear keep going in, even now.
Past cerebellum, spine, pituitary gland, veins, nerves, stem cells,
after going between my bones, between my memories, between my
    organs,
Agatha, without a scar,
although used language leaves no trace of having passed once used,
I belatedly feel that I am still living by the sound of the knife passing
    painfully,
as the gap widens, the oddly shaped knives vanish
Agatha, the morning-glory-shaped knife, the book-shaped knife, the
    cone-shaped knife,
the foot-shaped knife, these vulgar extensions of knives roam inside
    my body.
It seems you have now begun your journey through the pitfalls of old
    age and sickness,
this morning, the sight of me putting on shoes with the help of that
    vulgar knife.
Although so much time has passed, so far no news has come.

Voices Turned into Pottery

—Heavy snow warning

Because of an excess of love, the roof collapsed.
The voices of shadows emerging at length like pottery from vocal cords.

Clouds in the sky with cold air blasting holes.
Land of white pigs' teeth, white as pigs' voices.
The tiny mouths of mice frozen between dark gray toes.
How much did they gnaw, as if grumbling as they came? Are they
    indifferent
to haggard holes and worlds?
Time's tails, slothful consciousness over snow trash.

18-story ladder-trucks do handstands up to the clouds.

Purple lips putting icy air into the mouth.
Even playful death on its way to the abyss made by adults is not cold.
It becomes an extinct spot hiding chicken ribs beneath the wings.

In order to reflect always on others' lives,
rumbling, the sky began a fist-sized snow-fall.
The weather-station frozen white inside the eyes of freeze-dried pollock
like icicles hanging
from ancient colds.
Cough, cough. A folding screen of snow-clouds in the mountains
smashes a blizzard warning.

Huge banners announcing blizzard warnings
flapping, flapping, the white pottery voices of frozen pigs;
because of an excess of love, a pigsty where mice also lived collapsed.

On a Branch

We have to fall away from flower buds if we want to go there.
Painfully, like stars,
we have left fruit where we once had been.
Far, far away
those fruits are striving to remember us,
saying: We can't remember well, can't know that place.
But
we can't go back there again.
Though we want to bring those wounds with us, we can't.

Flower Rising in Tree Rings

Once the snow melts, the multitude of waterdrops in a red pine's xylem
start responding.
Inside there is one single flower that refuses to rise.
Aware of the flower's resolve not to rise, the owner
presses down on the calf-shaped bulbil to prevent it rising from the navel.
Only one single unknown flower that yields to all the other flowers
does not open its soul at the dizzying tip of a branch.
It cries like a frost flower on a cycad. Language of ice that never blossoms,
though all flowers standing with one single flower inside their breasts
eventually blossom, it changes its body in the xylem,
rising then going back down again.
At the very moment when numerous flowers are being hurt outside,
one tooth-like wild flower that never bloooms to perish or vanish,
placing that unutterable name which exists inside the red pine
in the xylem during the midnight snowfall,
one single flower freezes white like ice-porcelain.
Ah, inside the ice the flower is racing ahead like a roar.

I Commemorate Devastation

I have already begun my devastation.
I don't know how far this devastation will take me.
Revising a poem is harder than revising myself.
Long ago, since nothing could be compared to a poem,
though numerous lives might lie ahead of me,
they were less than one unfinished poem.
The excuse is that poetry is not being written any more.
Illusion will make me wander with infinite temptations,
and you will be stuck in the ditch of some metaphor.
Near the ventricles swinging constantly, noisy silences outside,
the bawling of intestines temporarily sewn up,
what are you going to do about such things?
Have you thought how they are going to survive?
Names that have disappeared from the lower parts of dreaming things,
language like uncorrected medical records, postpositions, final endings,
writing a poem is sure to leave a wound.
Nevertheless I keep transforming myself.
Once I forecast I would arrive first at a station you would not get off at,
and set off before anyone else,
but finally devastation is the irremediable reversion of a poem,
the place I will reach will just be my devastated insides
and here nameless flowers will bloom.
So I am hiding my face and breathing,
buried at the back of the poetic world.

Skyscraper Love Chain

The love chain was swinging, surely. You all thought,
that afternoon when a shadow passed near my eyelashes,
that day reflected five-colored clouds in the window
as it crossed the water by the stone bridge.
Once a dream had penetrated a leaf's cells at the end of a wretched
    summer,
it was left open for worms to pass the hole, surely.
Even though it gains a fistful of soil for days gone by,
the top of the skyscraper stays hidden in clouds, surely.
In vague memories like a moon buried in the sky,
the little face of a child opening a window and shouting.
Look! Here it's dead and gone! Leaves at the waterside
living by windows which never open,
leaf fins of slithery salmon-land, eyes and tongues
writing down a spiderwort alphabet.
A bright light comes in. Palms only as eyes.
While the meaning of the voices of leave-cells and ticklish writing all
    summer long
have been plated green.
You all knew already, surely.
that lights, not accumulating, penetrated my palms then left,
that I sent away water like wind in the sky,
that was a language that could not be spoken.
I say I remember those things, still opening and closing the air even now,
I say the light of the love chain has been sick since then.
The spiderwort disappeared in early winter winds,
and the love chain turned to face the sun by a window on the
    skyscraper.

Crazy About Mitochondria

One remote spring day
dreams of the mitochondria I learned about from the new semes-
    ter's textbook
are flapping torn wings in the twilight.
The fact that they had come visiting unexpectedly from somewhere,
days when I longed to stuff my injured face into a mirror with its
    back to the yard
on the wood-floored porch of a house where nobody lived, ancient
    Seoul with its lengthy future,
I have never seen any of you.
Aeogae's thirst where flowers and leaves emerge together
since they are living like evening, like grass,
the closed library, near
across the road faded red pavement blocks,
mirage-like fragments of mitochondria fine as dust go flying.
Spring nights, on the roofs of every car coming in, going back,
inside such sad time when the dead walk
you multiple mitochondrias
Headlights are bright, taillights are sad, right?
No, they're not sad.
Mitochondrias breathing inside completely forgotten textbooks.
Mesh shadows,
roll-calls of silence, caught in the retina, tear in passing.

A Camel in a Needle's Eye

Now I am passing through a needle's eye.
The tedious head has just about managed to emerge,
but the shoulders cannot not get through.
So a Bactrian camel is caught in a needle's eye.
Grim tragedy has finally turned into a joke.
This time the needle seems not to have good luck.
Like my destiny, it seems unable to let my body through this time.
I walk off, dragging the needle along.
The needle is pricking hard at my neck and waist.
I look outside. The clouds are idle. At times the earth
produces a clear autumn like this. Just as in the early Joseon dynasty
when the Korean alphabet was invented, or some such days,
the winds which have emerged from the needle's eye
are chewing at the white granite stones which once formed the food
    of the gods.
Again, one shoulder will not come through.
Eyes, ears, lips, hands all went through
but that one shoulder behind me will not come out.
Alas, a chubby Bactrian camel is caught in a needle.
My original goal was not one kilometer ahead.
So I will go on living, stuck like this in a needle.
Once I am done with living, only the needle will be left behind.
Nobody will remember the fact
that this needle's eye was the place my body was stuck.
Thinking of death and vividly alive,
I went my way with the needle round my neck like a necklace.
See my wonderful needle necklace,
see me stuck awkwardly in the needle's eye, unable to get out.
Now I am stuck in a needle's eye.

Please Grow Old like the Roots of a Tree

Self-portrait

Myself, elderly, sitting silent behind the door after the sun has set and
dusk has darkened.
Myself in the dark looking out at the chaos as twilight is deafened by
people chattering.
Myself grasping a bent cucumber, unable to eat it all in one day, just
clutching it.
Will old bones spend time somewhere, nibbling dried bread, I wonder?
Myself, holding my breath, breathing in and out as if I did not exist now.
A few clear-sighted people will realize that such days come inside morn-
ings then go away.

Could You Step Aside a Little?

The private life of a spiderwort–Part 2

Just enough sunlight came in for the shape of my leaves. The amount
of light that touched my eyes was bright and pure.
About the time when shade-loving plants underground kept coughing
plants would get torn, streams used to scream.
Weeds open their eyes in surprise as if a bird just flew away,
but they are beings that must be protected without equipment,
only leaves shaped like the curved shell of an egg.
No matter how many sunbeams pour down from the sky,
the only amount I need is the form of my leaves.
I don't have to receive all those many lights.
Don't say there's a handful or so of darkness inside my stalk.
Do not predict that death is hidden there.
I am an annual, I never winter with you.
Look! I come back to you after death.
I only remember this: I'll return into freezing winter,
hard ground that cannot even open its eyes. Soil and roots,
merely a growing point, patterns of memory.
The sunshine always only enters through the surface of leaves.
And although it sometimes grows darker or brighter,
my thin film has feeling through sensitive pores.
Wait, excuse me! Could you step aside a little?

I Am Not in Erdene Zuu Monastery

I am not now in Erdene Zuu Monastery.*
This sentence is not valid and suggests nothing poetic.
Saying that I am not now in Erdene Zuu Monastery
is to imagine the unimaginable, and that is an ever-repeated problem.
But I am in Erdene Zuu Monastery.
There's no way of proving it but I am in Erdene Zuu Monastery.
I tried thinking of someone in Erdene Zuu Monastery
thinking of Erdene Zuu Monastery
but thinking 'I am not now in Erdene Zuu Monastery,'
but I could not, so I stopped trying.
They are cleverly escaping between my distant thoughts.
I'm always like that, never mind the validity of the sentence.
I just cannot get out of the difficulty of this thought as such.
Do I really have to validate saying that I am not in Erdene Zuu
    Monastery?
As I walk along, all alone, I am engrossed in that thought.
To be frank, I am now in Erdene Zuu Monastery
as if I were in Erdene Zuu Monastery.
Of course, saying that I am in Erdene Zuu Monastery
is just the same as saying that Erdene Zuu Monastery does not exist
Saying that for me Erdene Zuu Monastery is,
and is not, can be presented as equally problematic.
The problem comes with having a problem with the fact that nothing is.
But the I who am not in Erdene Zuu Monastery is so very lonesome.
The course is that of anyone suffering as they adjust to the melody.
Why am I thinking of the I not in Erdene Zuu Monastery?
Every time I think of that sentence I grow sad.
Where is the I wandering who am not in Erdene Zuu Monastery?
And as for you, why are you not in Erdene Zuu Monastery?
Let me now, at this moment, be staying in Erdene Zuu Monastery.
Since I have no goal, I look lonely like a tree.
Like a mountain at the entrance to a desert where I am not, I gaze at
    the sky.

---

* The Erdene Zuu Monastery is the name of a temple built in Mongolia in
1586.

Like a dazzling cloud appearing in the sky of Erdene Zuu
    Monastery
I am unable to say anything.

Looking at the Deep Blue Sky

I feel as though the sky's club is about to strike my head.
If the pain passes in a flash, a moment,
it is right for me to say I'm waiting for the club.
If there is a moment the club never thought of, let that
be the time for it to cut the cord and rush through the air at the
    speed of light.
Come on, club, smash my head with a single blow
Do not quietly leave my head swollen like a watermelon.
The club will then waft away to the distant sky
and your reality will spend the summer in perfect peace.
It leaves no sign at all that it scraped across my empty head
like a swing, like an autumn swing with nobody on it.
Club rolling in the chill wind, my own gigantic club!
Tear up and burn old tracks, old tensions,
pull out all my guts, hang them up in the sky like seaweed
so that the earth can cross over at ease, I mean it.
In that dry sky, thunder and lightning are rumbling.
Today I once more look up at an empty sky. Impatient club!
You horror-struck, tearful, one-off club!
One tremendous, piercing club with the speed of light.

Blue Ice Fish

Are you familiar with blue ice? Have you ever stood alone, leaning back,
and seen simultaneously that dark city, the afternoon of that gray city
of humanity speeding through eternity and the moment
when countless millions of window panes glitter in sunlight from on high?

The earth from which, alas, blue ice has vanished, alas,
the corrupt, deformed earth, and have you seen waves in the long vapor
    trails
of icy cumulus clouds? Do you recall the dawn sky or
the Far East's golden twilight glow as the sun sets in the West?

I long to munch blue ice; is there any blue ice?
I want to go sliding over blue ice, but
blue ice is a dinosaur, it's weeping like a dinosaur, like a soul,
but then again, the impossibility of washing every dirty hand. . . .

Does the city really believe in blue ice? Do you believe it exists?
Lakes frozen as blue gems, the gray city,
cold mornings when blue fish swam past beneath that ice,
ah, city, the fishes' eyes are frozen, as blue light

Black Death Suddenly Hurled into a Labyrinth

There is something called death's labyrinth. I suddenly entered that
    labyrinth then stopped.
One black corpse entering at the speed of light like a headlight beam
    beneath the car,
under the driving seat.

One mass of black chaos, not breathing, remained
sitting in the middle of the road. The expelled breath seemed about to
    explode.
All the veins and blood vessels, the capillaries of the cranial reflexes
    taken aback,
in the still, utter darkness many vehicles were passing.

No emergency calls reached the control center from anywhere.
And no nearby mind or text reached our star outside the earth.
Here, as I confronted squarely the break in communications
I glimpsed a light-bundle rushing like a momentary flood
into the labyrinth of the truth of non-communication.
That was the corpse's swansong.

Ah, breathtaking, the swan's swansong, no sign of a phosphate group,
I was like the thirst of the water ceasing to exist as it was sucked into
    last summer's branches.
Speak, speak, leap out, leap out,
where have you gone, blankly forgetting life, losing your body? The giant
squatted kneeling in the road like a mountain of darkness. As if that was
    what death was,
as if it were a place for someone precariously sitting in the lotus
    position,
the news that father had died somewhere on the road just before reach-
    ing home, supper under a lamp, in the dark up a mountain.

I was speeding toward Seoul along endless intestines, as if running
    away. . . .
like one guilty of a collision.
Unfortunately, the subject of this death was glimpsed from behind on
    the other side.

Jaguar in the City Center One Clear Day

One jaguar is walking along. It looks back.
It has heard the sound of poetic diction returning to silence.
Instinct suggests that there is an inspiration following it
so, just once, it looks back.
Autumn flaming at the tips of reeds
floods across the city center's main street. When all lose heart
the jaguar, with a superb upright physique,
goes walking on four feet into eternal autumn. Coming to this city for
the first time,
that rambling course impossible to remember,
lightly brushing over its clothing, a smell of dried grass,
the jaguar's back tattooed with red leaves of sunlight,
quite at a loss.
The sharp teeth inside the narrow lips, the black pattern with red spots,
and inside the unseen intestines too, the hue of autumn,
a gray boundary, the entrance to the underground bookstore
at the end of the ten-lane highway,
the jaguar vanishes completely.

Grass and Apartments

The sky is completely full of apartment lights.
There is no apartment for a foreign family with triangular noses.
A wind swing
where women's and children's laundry is swinging.
A balcony where sunshine never set foot.
A door that even wind could never open is firmly closed.

Dew has come down to the sky of grass and lives like stars.
Indeed,
staring at the apartments, lengthy time shatters into pieces.
That woman
must be living somewhere at a latitude of about 37 degrees North
in the capital of South Korea, where gloomy, icy clouds are blowing past.

An apartment a grasshopper and a mantis are renting
rotates with mountains in the blue sky, then comes back.
Occasionally reaching out a hand to pluck and eat clouds,
weeds live with the wind on the apartment rooftop.

A Counterfeit Banknote

I have a counterfeit banknote.
The counterfeit stares up at me
as I look down at the counterfeit. It suspects me. I feel unwell.
It has passed through numerous banks, markets, mornings,

I open it out, open it out, but who made it?
I treasure it as time's perjury.
When I feel depressed, I slyly take it out on the steps of an
    underpass.
Without anyone noticing, I hold up the thin paper glass plate to
    the sunlight.
The other side shows through, then disappears.

The counterfeit note does not recognize itself.
It never mistakes itself for some hopeful prognosis,
eccentric symbol or meaning.
For the counterfeit is essentially a counterfeit.
Once all evaluations and values have collapsed,
the metaphor of this banknote will disappear like a flame.

Inside myself, a mysterious organism is moving.
Inside the counterfeit banknote, there is a counterfeit banknote.

Summer Devours Wife

I calm the desire that has reached skyscraper level.
The color of the desire is white, red, black, dark blue.
No one is able to control this desire.
A wife is wailing in an apartment.

The wife has strong instincts. The wife is young.
The wife, pregnant with a baby,
is having the baby cut out, hanging upside down from a ring in the
    air.
With the cries of dying children on a grassy field,
a day's universe is passing.

Desire wants to vomit out desire and erase it.
It wants to become the desire of desire.
Dreaming summer is dying inside summer.
At the peak season of desire, the wife is dying, too.

Desire is once again slowly climbing up onto the rooftops.
Every year the wife is devoured by summer.

My Momentary Toy

Do not call me by a name.
Do not try to bind me inside your name.
If you have your own way to go, please go your way.
Do not try to take me with you.
We have been calling each other by name for far too long.
I want to call out my name into chaos.
It is not clear yet
but it seems you might need some oblivion too.
It's as if I want to get rid of need.
Even though I came as a cloud, as wind, another morning's flowers
other than some promise of daybreak,
now we must go back and look inside the time before we met.
These words too should be forgotten,
but I want the present to be the present of a distant past.
Do not try to show me everything.
It's alright now for you not to do so.
Let me be myself alone.
Let me bask silently in sunshine at the foot of a wall.
I am telling you far too ancient words
at a bus-stop in the west of the city at sunset.

About the Author

Ko Hyeong-ryeol was born in 1954 in Sokcho, Gangwon-do, on the East coast of Korea just south of the DMZ, at the foot of Mount Seorak. After leaving high school he began to work as a manual laborer in Jeju Island, breaking stones for the construction of a highway. In 1974 his father died and he had to take responsibility for his family so he returned to Sokcho and became a clerk in the office of a small rural district nearby. After eight years, already recognized as a poet, he went up to Seoul and in 1985 began to work as Editor-in-Chief responsible for poetry in the Changbi publishing company. He held this position for some twenty years before retiring in 2005. He now lives in Yangpyeong, to the east of Seoul.

Photograph of the author by Ko Jung-Cheol. Used by permission.

He published his first poems in the review *Hyeondae munhak* (Contemporary Literature) in 1979. He has published multiple volumes of poetry, including *Daecheongbong subakbat* (The Watermelon Patch at the Top of Daecheong Peak, 1985); *Haecheong* (Hawk, 1987); *Sajilli daeseol* (Heavy Snow in Sajin-ri, 1993); the long narrative poem *Little Boy* (1995); *Seongekkot nunbucheo* (Frost Flowers Reflected in my Eyes, 1998); *Gimpo Unhogadeunjipeseo* (In Unho Garden at Gimpo, 2001); *Pam Misiryeong* (Misiryeong by Night, 2006); the long narrative poem *Bungsae* (The Great Roc, 2010); *Naneun Ereudenjo sawone opda* (I am not in Erdene Zuu Temple, 2010); *Yurichereul tonggwahada* (I Pass through an Educt, 2012); *Jigureul iseungira bulleujulkka* (Shall I Call the Earth this World? 2013); *Amudo chajaoji anneun geourida* (I am a Mirror Nobody Visits, 2015); a volume of essays *Eunbit mulgogi* (Silver Salmon, 1999) and a volume of poems for children *Ppang teulgo janeun eonni* (Sister Asleep Holding Bread, 2001).

He has received a number of awards, including the 55th Modern Literary Award; the Baekseok Award; the Jihun Literary Award; the Republic of Korea Culture and Arts Award; the Hyeongpyeong Literary Award. He was the chief editor of the magazine *Sipyeong* from 2000 until 2013; from 2000 he played a leading role in organizing and participating in the activities of the "Korea-ASEAN Poets' Literature Festival." He is currently chief editor of the review *Hyeondae Sihak* (Modern Poetry).

About the Translators

Brother Anthony of Taizé was born in Cornwall in 1942. He has been living in Korea since 1980. He is an Emeritus Professor of Sogang University (Seoul) and Chair-Professor at Dankook University. He is currently President of the Royal Asiatic Society Korea Branch. He has published some forty volumes of translations of Korean literature, mostly poetry, including ten volumes of works by Ko Un. He took Korean citizenship in 1994. An Sonjae is his official Korean name. He received the Korean government's Award of Merit in October 2008 for promoting knowledge of Korean literature in the world. In 2015 he was awarded an honorary MBE by Queen Elizabeth for his contributions to Korea-British relations. His home page is http://anthony.sogang.ac.kr/

Lee Hyung-Jin received his doctorate in comparative literature at Penn State University and is a professor of translation studies in the School of English at Sookmyung Women's University, in Seoul. His translations of Korean poetry include *Walking on a Washing Line: Poems of Kim Seung-hee*.

www.ingramcontent.com/pod-product-compliance
Lightning Source LLC
Chambersburg PA
CBHW022012090426

42741CB00007B/1001